My Favorite CHANUKAH
Activity & Coloring Book

Illustrated By: **Arthur Friedman**

©1996 Jewish Educational Toys
P.O. Box 250469
Brooklyn, New York 11225

Help Leah & David through this menorah maze to the Chanukah gelt.

Help the children get their gifts. Follow the dreidle, latke and candle squares in order, by only going up and down, or right and left.

We Celebrate Chanukah for eight days!
Help David find the eight candles.

Find the following words in the word block below moving up, down, left, right and diagonally.

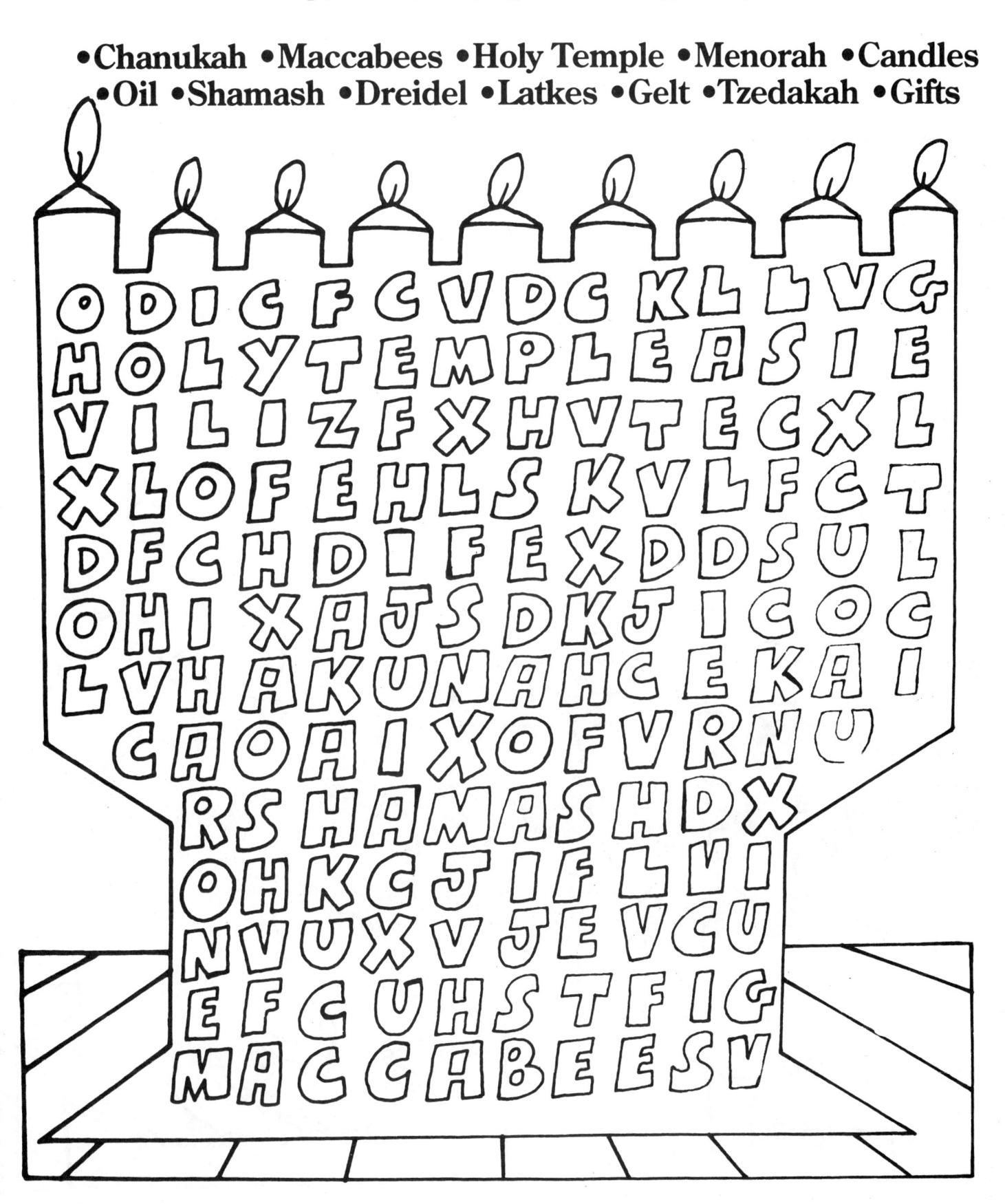

- **Chanukah** • **Maccabees** • **Holy Temple** • **Menorah** • **Candles**
- **Oil** • **Shamash** • **Dreidel** • **Latkes** • **Gelt** • **Tzedakah** • **Gifts**

```
O D I C F C V D C K L L V G
H O L Y T E M P L E A S I E
V I L I Z F X H V T E C X L
X L O F E H L S K V L F C T
D F C H D I F E X D D S U L
O H I X A J S D K J I C O C
L V H A K U N A H C E K A I
C A O A I X O F V R N U
R S H A M A S H D X
O H K C J I F L V I
N V U X V J E V C U
E F C U H S T F I G
M A C C A B E E S V
```

Complete the Dot-To-Dot to find out
What you can't do without on Chanukah.

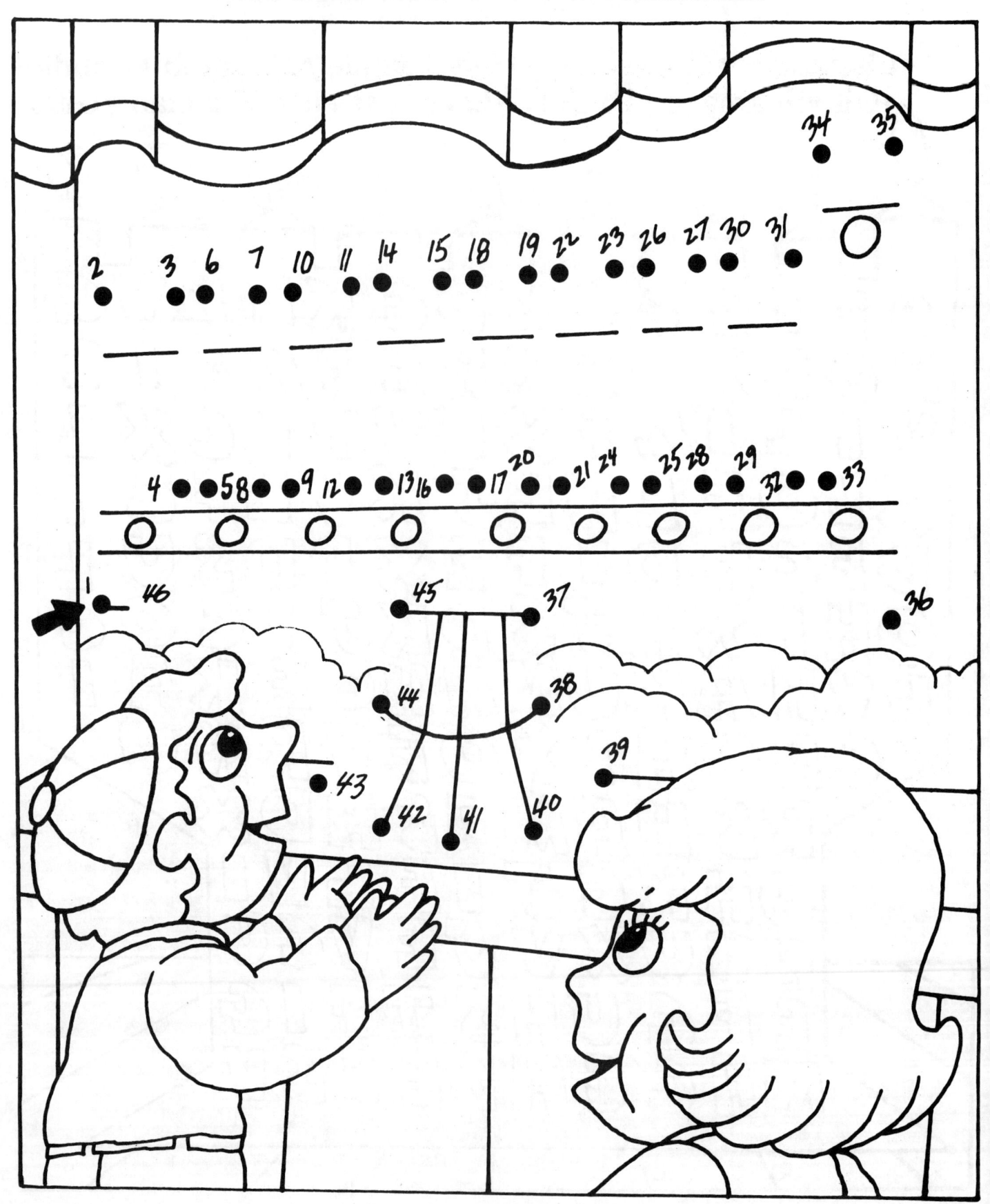

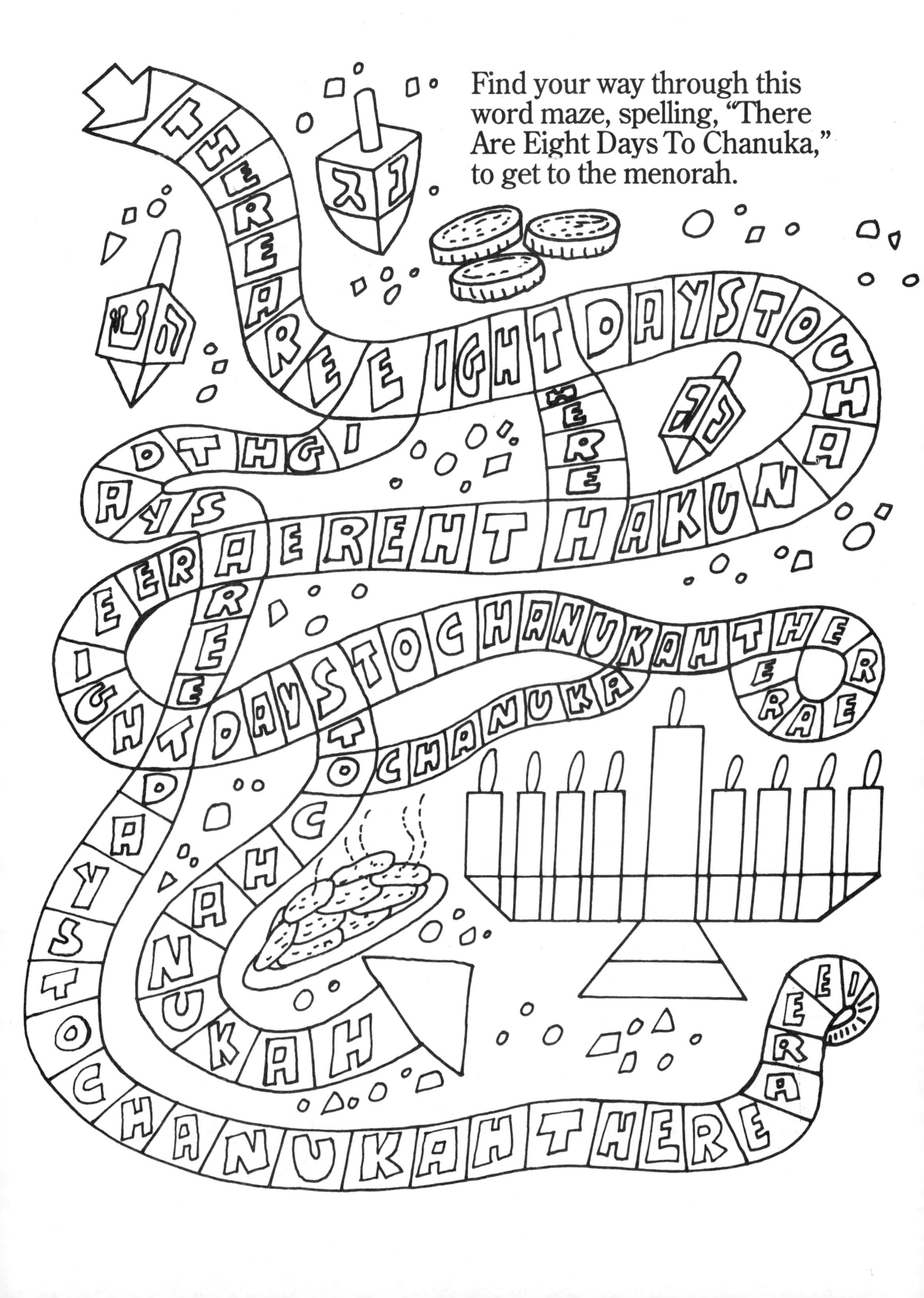

Find your way through this word maze, spelling, "There Are Eight Days To Chanuka," to get to the menorah.

Color-By-Number

**1-Brown • 2-Orange • 3-Purple • 4-Blue • 5-Yellow
6-Pink • 7-Bright Green • 8-Red**

Using the pictures as clues, write in the correct answers to this crossword puzzle.

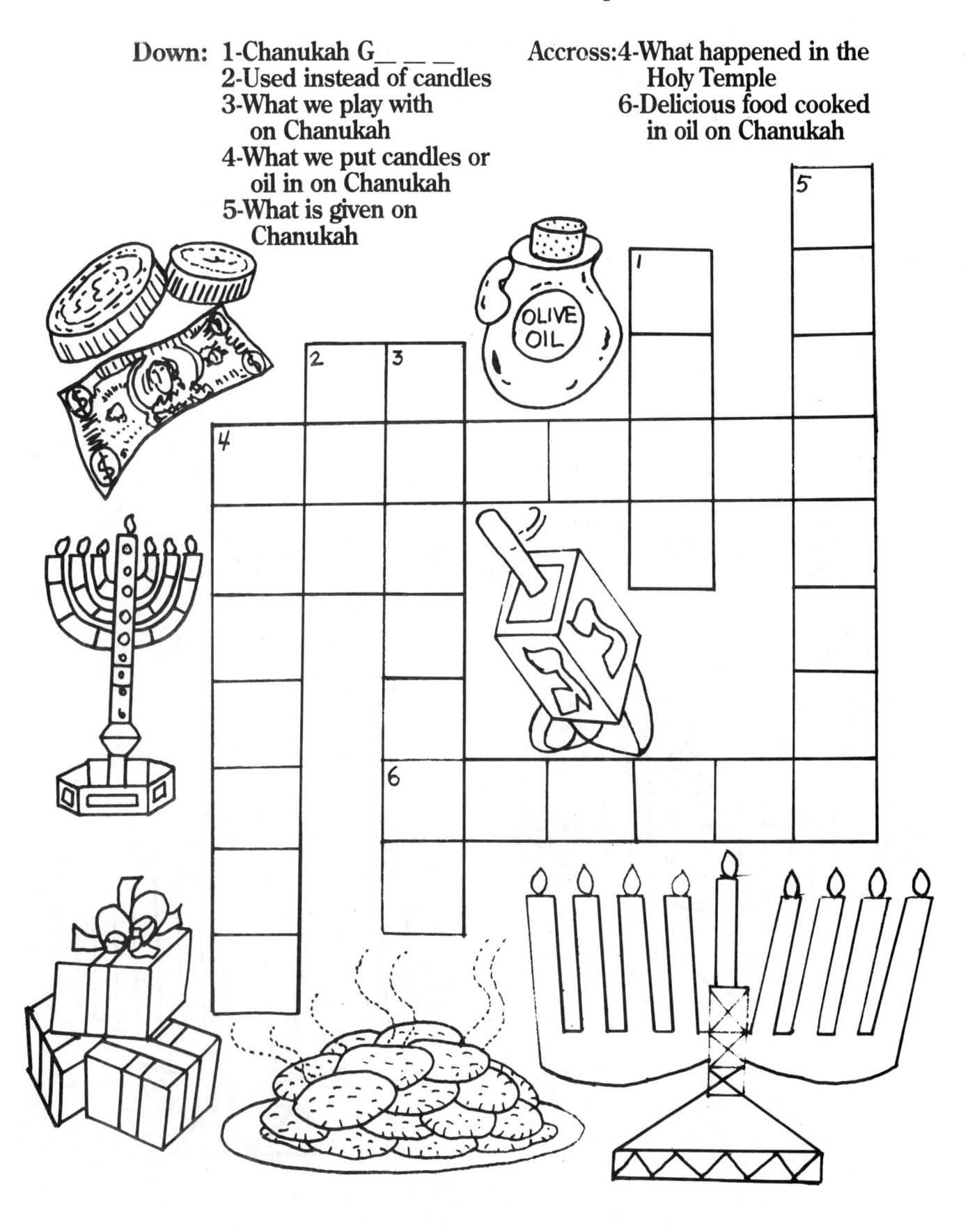

Down:
1. Chanukah G_ _ _
2. Used instead of candles
3. What we play with on Chanukah
4. What we put candles or oil in on Chanukah
5. What is given on Chanukah

Accross:
4. What happened in the Holy Temple
6. Delicious food cooked in oil on Chanukah

Which menorah is different from all the rest?

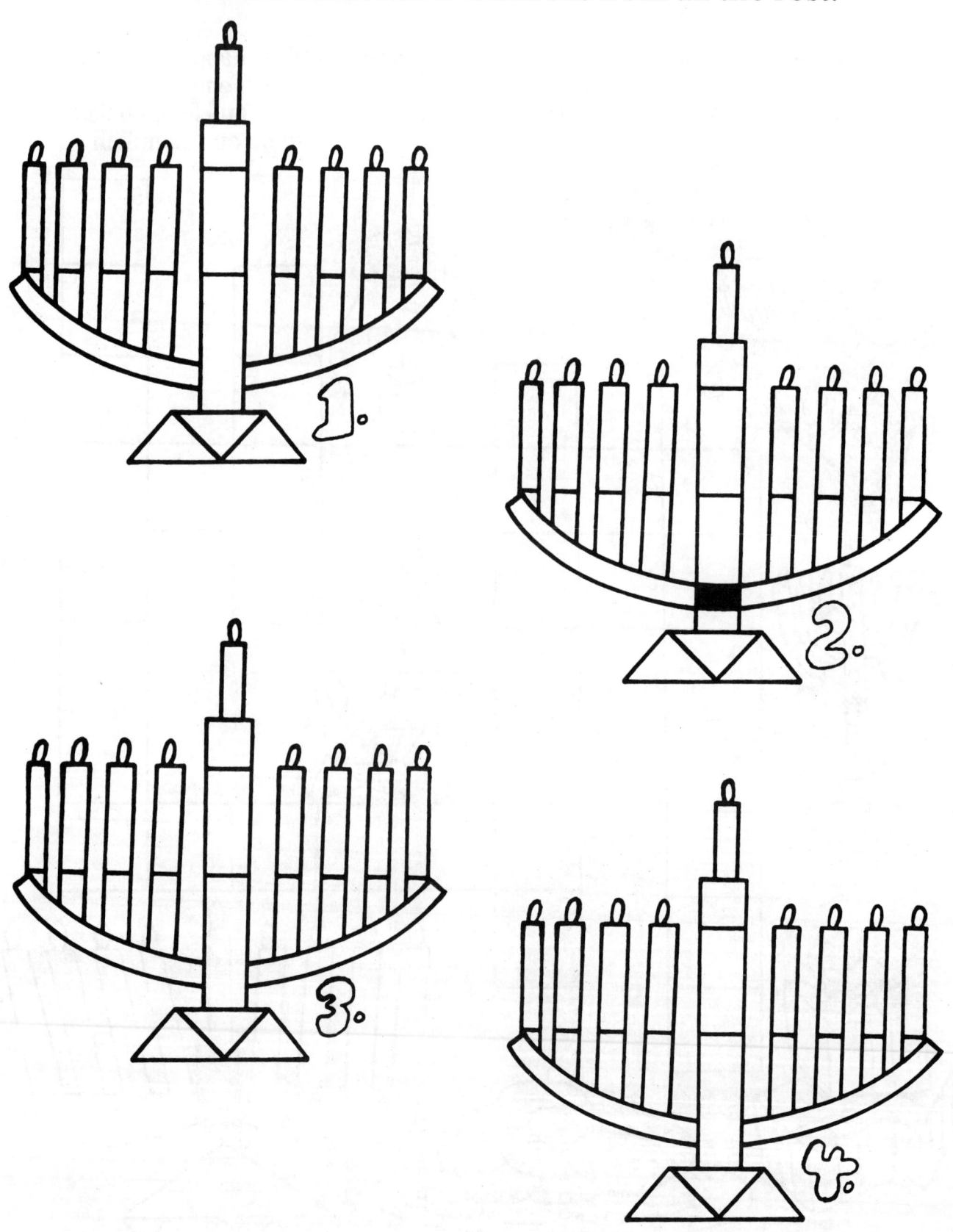

1.

2.

3.

4.

Picture Puzzle: Cut each box carefully and put them together correctly to form a Chanukah picture.

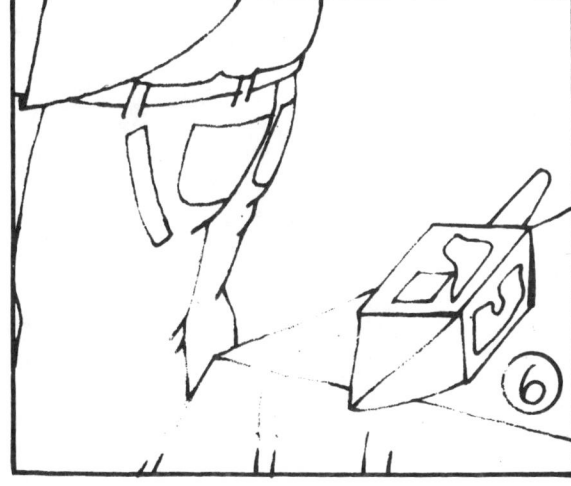

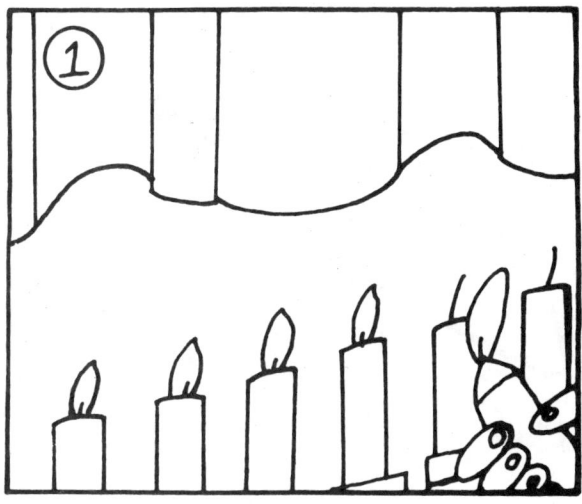

Match each dreidel in the left column to its shadow in the right column by drawing a line.

Circle the seven things that are wrong in this Chanukah picture.

Complete the rebus to find three main highlights of Chanukah.

Help the children through the latke maze to get to those delicious latkes.

Dot-To-Dot

By going only up, down, right and left, follow the order of נגהש through this picture maze and help the children to the delicious latkes.

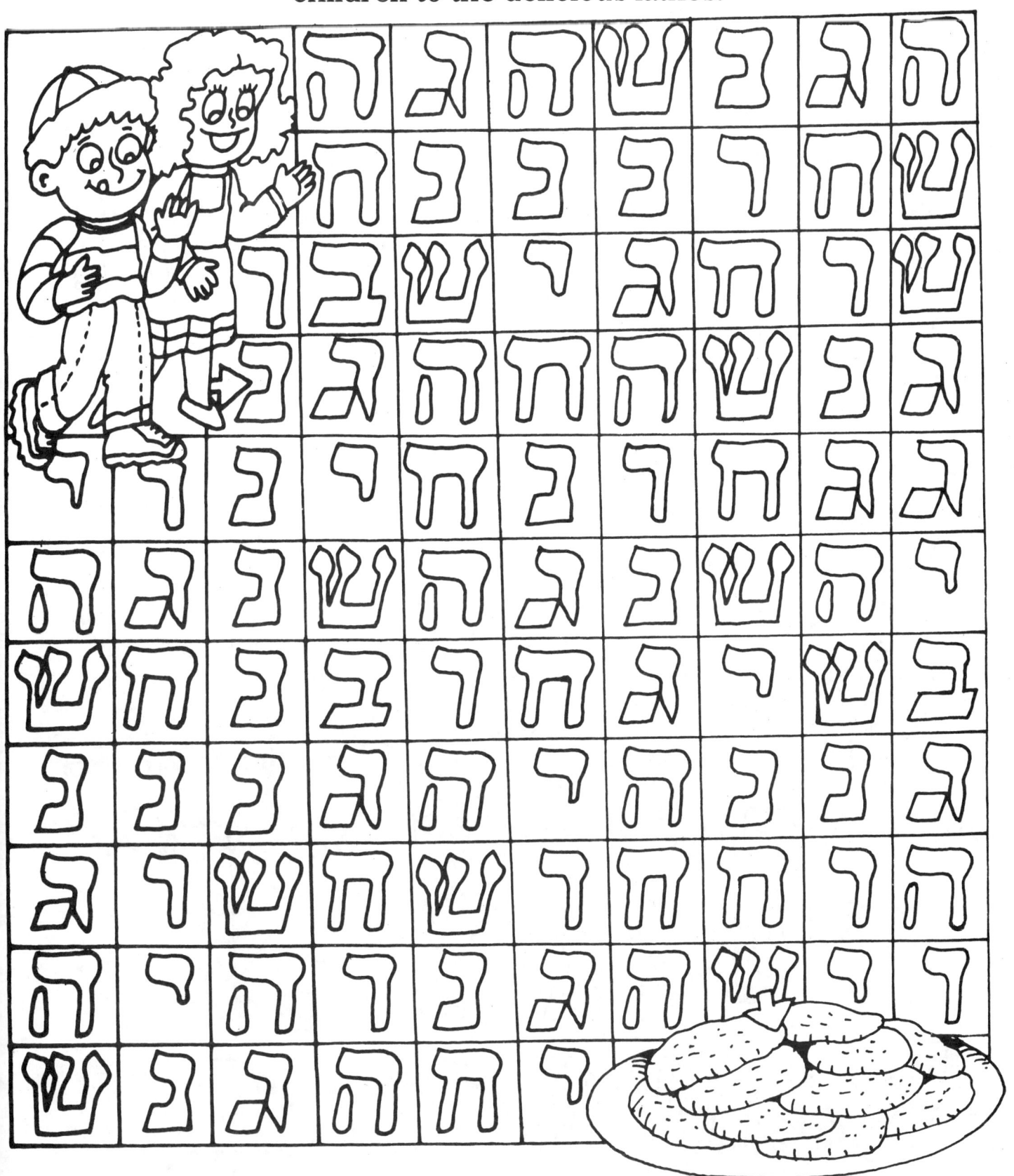

Help the children thru this word maze spelling "A Great Miracle Happened There," to get to the menorah in the Holy Temple.

Color in the shapes with a dot to reveal a hidden picture.

Follow each letter, with its line, to the empty boxes below to spell a greeting on this holiday.

P Y A P H

K N H A H C A U

Color By Number

1-Blue • 2-Dark Green • 3-Light Green • 4-Pink • 5-Red
6-Yellow • 7-Purple • 8-Orange • 9-Brown • 10-Tan

Which two dreidles are the same?

Picture Puzzle: Cut each box carefully and put them together correctly to form a Chanukah picture.

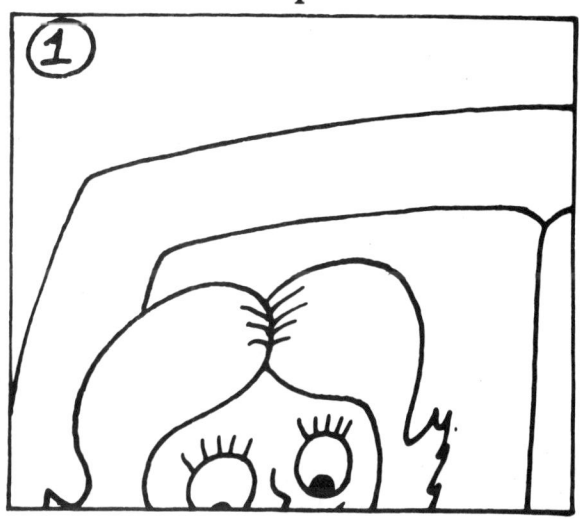

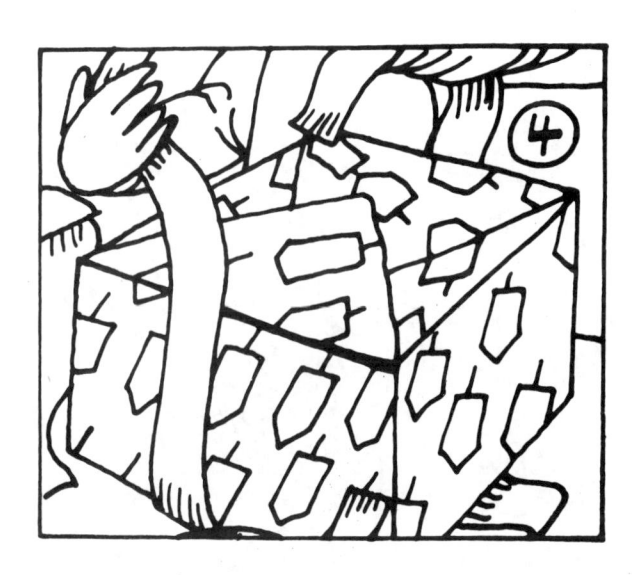

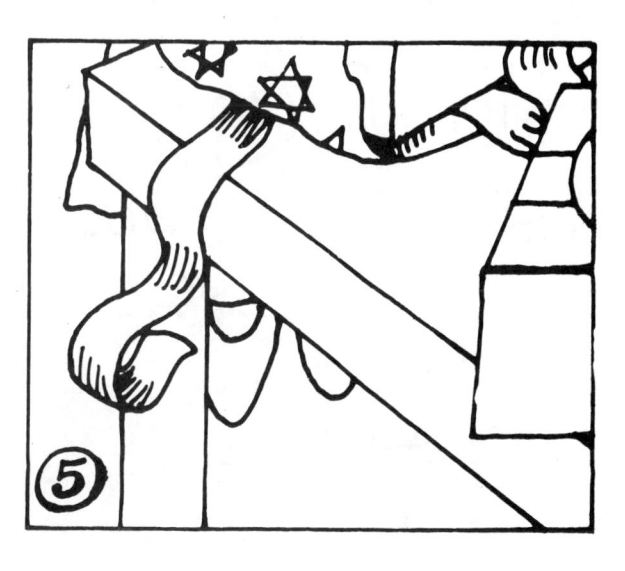

Circle the six things that are wrong in this Chanukah picture.

Find the following words in the word block below, moving up, down, right, left and diagonally.
"A GREAT MIRACLE HAPPENED THERE."

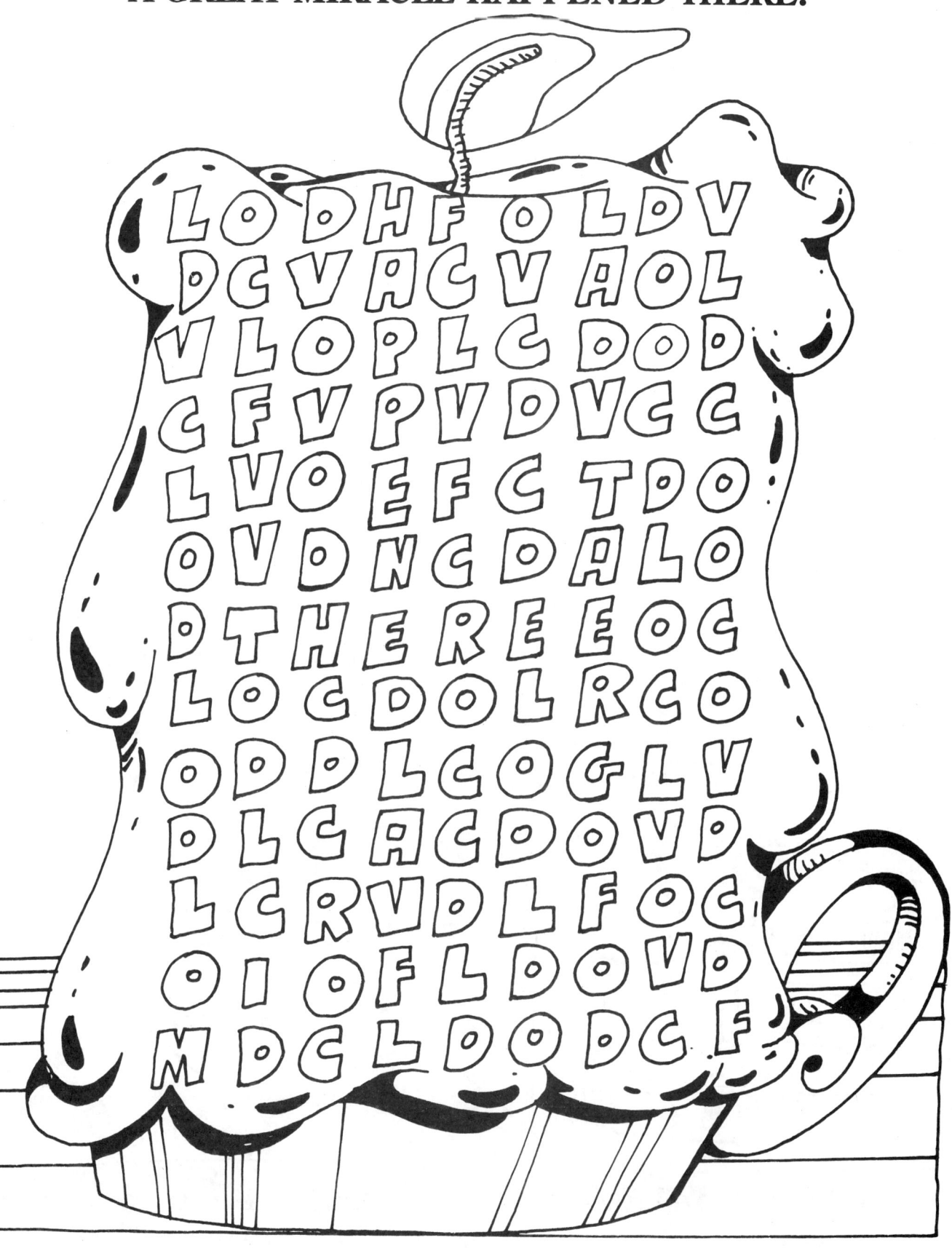

```
L O D H F O L D V
D C V A C V A O L
V L O P L C D O D
C F V P V D V C C
L V O E F C T D O
O V D N C D A L O
D T H E R E E O C
L O C D O L R C O
O D D L C O G L V
D L C A C D O V D
L C R V D L F O C
O I O F L D O V D
M D C L D O D C F
```

Color-By-Number

**1-Yellow • 2-Yellow/Orange • 3-Orange • 4-Red • 5-Magenta
6-Light Green • 7-Green • 8-Blue • 9-Purple • 10-Brown**

Find the eight hidden dreidles.

Color in the spaces with a dot to reveal a Chanuka picture.

Dot-To-Dot

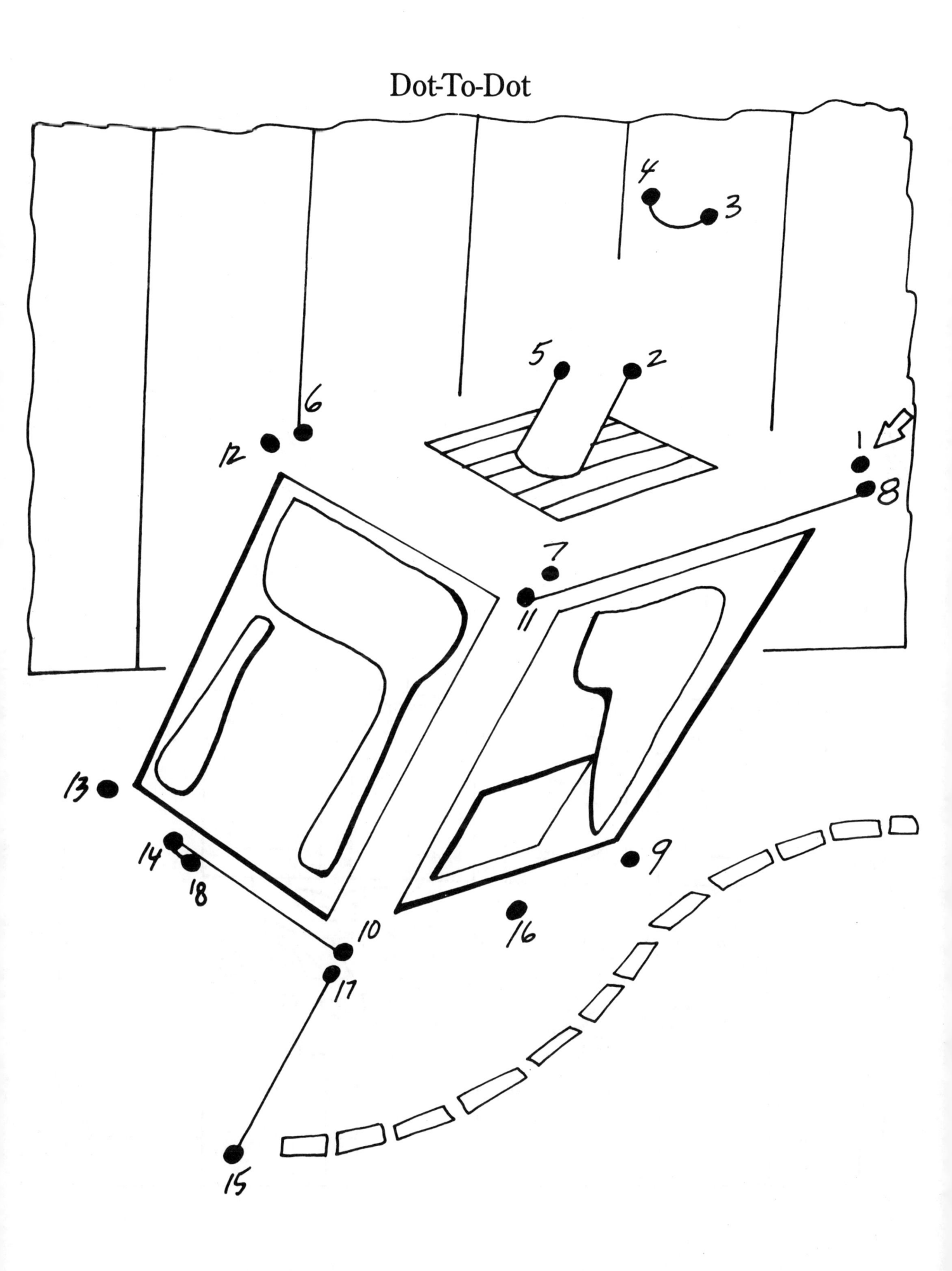

Follow each letter, with its line, to the empty boxes below to spell some main objects given on Chanukah.

T S G I F

L G T E

Copy the picture, in the top box, into the box below.

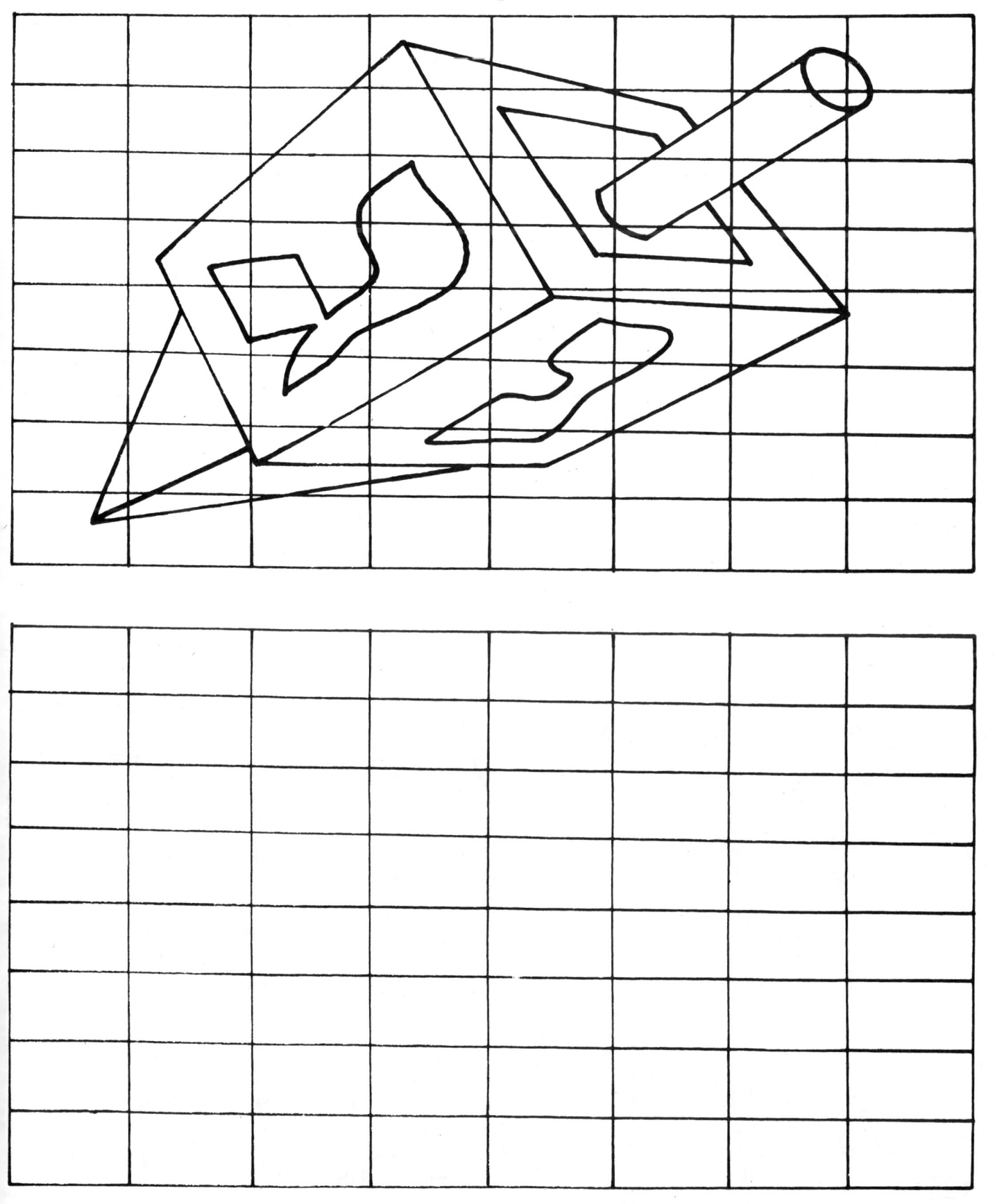

Find the hidden latkes.